T0306615

OCCASIONAL PAPER

The 2008 Battle of Sadr City

David E. Johnson • M. Wade Markel • Brian Shannon

Prepared for the United States Army

Approved for public release; distribution unlimited

ARROYO CENTER

The research described in this report was sponsored by the United States Army under Contract No. W74V8H-06-C-0001.

Library of Congress Cataloging-in-Publication Data is available for this publication.

ISBN 978-0-8330-5301-5

The RAND Corporation is a nonprofit institution that helps improve policy and decisionmaking through research and analysis. RAND's publications do not necessarily reflect the opinions of its research clients and sponsors.

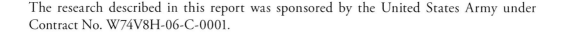 is a registered trademark.

Published 2011 by the RAND Corporation
1776 Main Street, P.O. Box 2138, Santa Monica, CA 90407-2138
1200 South Hayes Street, Arlington, VA 22202-5050
4570 Fifth Avenue, Suite 600, Pittsburgh, PA 15213-2665
RAND URL: http://www.rand.org/
To order RAND documents or to obtain additional information, contact
Distribution Services: Telephone: (310) 451-7002;
Fax: (310) 451-6915; Email: order@rand.org

Preface

This paper was written as part of an ongoing project entitled "The Battle of Sadr City." The project aims to assess the U.S. operations, principally in spring and early summer 2008, to stop Shiite extremists from firing short-range rockets and mortars into the International Zone from Sadr City. This battle also set the conditions designed to allow stability and Iraqi government control to be extended to the whole of Baghdad.

This paper summarizes the research still in progress and is meant to provide insights and lessons learned from the Battle of Sadr City that can inform a broader understanding of urban operations—particularly those conducted as part of irregular warfare—and thereby help the Army understand what capabilities it will need in the future. The research results are not yet final. Another document will address topics discussed in this paper and should be useful to those seeking an in-depth examination of the Battle of Sadr City.

This research is sponsored by the Office of the Deputy Chief of Staff, G-8, Headquarters, Department of the Army, and is being conducted in RAND Arroyo Center's Strategy, Doctrine, and Resources Program. RAND Arroyo Center, part of the RAND Corporation, is a federally funded research and development center sponsored by the United States Army.

Questions and comments regarding this research are welcome and should be directed to the leader of the research team, David E. Johnson, at davidj@rand.org.

The Project Unique Identification Code (PUIC) for the project that produced this document is ASPMO09426.

For more information on RAND Arroyo Center, contact the Director of Operations (telephone 310-393-0411, extension 6419; FAX 310-451-6952; email Marcy_Agmon@rand.org), or visit Arroyo's website at http://www.rand.org/ard/.

Contents

Figures

Acknowledgments

This study began as the result of a conversation between several RAND Arroyo Center researchers and General John M. (Jack) Keane (U.S. Army, retired), former U.S. Army Vice Chief of Staff; Lieutenant General Robert P. Lennox, U.S. Army Deputy Chief of Staff, G-8; Lieutenant General William J. Lennox, Jr. (U.S. Army, retired), former Superintendent of the U.S. Military Academy at West Point; and Timothy Muchmore, Director of the U.S. Army Quadrennial Defense Review Office, G-8. We were discussing a then-recent Israeli operation in Gaza (Operation Cast Lead, which ended in January 2009). During the conversation, several participants noted that there were similarities between Cast Lead and a battle that coalition forces had fought in Iraq in 2008: the Battle of Sadr City. The RAND participants in the conversation had heard little of this operation. As we found during our subsequent research and discussions with broader audiences, the battle was only briefly noted and never fully analyzed. Through this project, we sought to make the battle and its effects more widely known and to document the lessons from Sadr City that we believe have great relevance for how the U.S. Army prepares for future operations.

We would like to acknowledge the two individuals who most understood the importance of this project and supported it throughout its course: Lieutenant General Robert P. Lennox and Timothy Muchmore. Dozens of participants in the battle also gave generously of their time in the form of interviews and follow-on discussions. Their accounts of their first-hand experiences in the events we describe in this paper were absolutely invaluable. Finally, the reviewers of this paper—Colonel Gian P. Gentile (faculty member at the U.S. Military Academy at West Point), Christopher G. Pernin (RAND Corporation), and David A. Shlapak (RAND Corporation)—provided thorough and very useful reviews.

The efforts of all these individuals contributed immeasurably to this product. We owe them all an enormous debt of gratitude.

Abbreviations

1-2 SCR	1st Squadron, 2nd Stryker Cavalry Regiment
3-4 BCT	3rd Brigade Combat Team, 4th Infantry Division
4ID	4th Infantry Division
AWT	aerial weapons team
BCT	brigade combat team
CAS	close air support
COIN	counterinsurgency
GMLRS	Guided Multiple Launch Rocket System
IED	improvised explosive device
ISF	Iraqi security forces
ISR	intelligence, surveillance, and reconnaissance
JAM	Jaish al-Mahdi
JSS	Joint Security Station
JSTARS	Joint Surveillance Target Attack Radar System
MNC-I	Multi-National Corps–Iraq
MND-B	Multi-National Division–Baghdad
MNF-I	Multi-National Force–Iraq
NP	National Police
PSDS2	persistent surveillance and dissemination of systems
RAID	Rapid Aerostat Initial Deployment
RPG	rocket-propelled grenade
SIGINT	signals intelligence
SOF	special operations forces
TOC	tactical operations center

UAS	unmanned aircraft system
UAV	unmanned aerial vehicle
TF 1-68 CAB	Task Force, 1st Combined Arms Battalion, 68th Armored Regiment

The 2008 Battle of Sadr City

Background

A team from RAND Arroyo Center is in the final stages of research on a project for the Office of the Deputy Chief of Staff, G-8, Headquarters, Department of the Army, entitled "The Battle of Sadr City." The purpose of this project is to provide insights and lessons learned from the Battle of Sadr City that can inform a broader understanding of urban operations and thereby help the U.S. Army evaluate what capabilities it may need in the future.

We know of no full analysis of the 2008 Battle of Sadr City. The action did attract some journalistic attention, mostly because of the extensive use of unmanned drones and other high-technology assets. Indeed, *60 Minutes* aired a segment on the battle.[1] However, the battle has received relatively little scholarly attention. The Institute for the Study of War published an accurate descriptive summary of the battle in August 2008, based mostly on press reports.[2] Other sources mention it in passing, interpreting its significance but without providing much underlying detail about its conduct. Irish journalist Patrick Cockburn attributes the outcome to Muqtada al-Sadr's political calculations, while Adeed Dawisha credits Prime Minister Nouri al-Maliki's resolute behavior with fostering a nonsectarian political climate. Neither have much to say about how the battle's conduct helped produce the resulting outcome.[3] Within U.S. military circles, such debate as has occurred has centered on the relative value of lethal force and reconstruction in counterinsurgency.[4] For the most part, however, there has been surprisingly little written that describes or analyzes the battle.

RAND's study aims to provide a more complete description of the battle (based on primary-source material), to analyze its outcome, and to derive implications for the U.S. Army's future conduct of land operations. This short paper describes our initial findings.

---

[1] Leslie Stahl, "The Battle of Sadr City," *60 Minutes*, October 12, 2008.

[2] Marisa Cochrane, *Special Groups Regenerate*, Washington, D.C.: Institute for the Study of War, 2008.

[3] Patrick Cockburn, *Moqtada al-Sadr and the Battle for the Future of Iraq*, New York: Scribner, 2008, pp. 98–106; Adeed Dawisha, "Iraq: A Vote Against Sectarianism," *Journal of Democracy*, Vol. 21, No. 3, July 2010, pp. 26–40. In a May 2010 article, Geraint Hughes does not even mention the battle, even though he notes the simultaneous battle in Basra (see Geraint Hughes, "The Insurgencies in Iraq, 2003–2009: Origins, Developments and Prospects," *Defence Studies*, Vol. 10, No. 1, May 2010, pp. 152–176).

[4] See, for example, Craig Collier, "Two Cheers for Lethal Operations," *Armed Forces Journal International*, August 2010.

Methodology

The Arroyo team used after-action reports, briefings, and other primary and secondary sources to research this paper. Our most valuable sources, however, were interviews conducted between August 2009 and April 2011 with a broad range of participants from the units involved in the following phases: the prebattle surge in the vicinity of Sadr City; the Battle of Sadr City; and the postbattle stabilization and reconstruction efforts. These participants ranged from lieutenants to the commanding general of the 4th Infantry Division. Our interviews were mostly with U.S. Army officers but also included a U.S. Air Force officer, a former Iraqi intelligence official, and U.S. government officials. These interviews provided critical information about not only what happened but *why* it happened.

Our understanding of the Sadrist militia comes from contemporary analyses by the International Crisis Group and other, similar organizations; from journalistic accounts; and from U.S. Army assessments. That said, this paper largely reflects assessments about the battle made by U.S. combatants.

Finally, we consciously decided, in conjunction with our sponsor, to write this paper at an unclassified level to enable its broad distribution. Unless otherwise noted, the information contained in this paper is derived from our interviews; in general, interviewees are not identified by name.

Setting Conditions

The 2008 Battle of Sadr City took place nearly 15 months after the beginning of the U.S. "surge" in Iraq. President George W. Bush stated the mission of U.S. forces when he announced the surge in a January 10, 2007, speech: "to help Iraqis clear and secure neighborhoods, to help them protect the local population, and to help ensure that the Iraqi forces left behind are capable of providing the security that Baghdad needs."[5] The "Baghdad Security Plan" was a key element of the surge. Its purpose was announced by Major General Joseph Fil, Jr., commander of the Multi-National Division–Baghdad (MND-B) on February 16, 2007:

> This new plan involves three basic parts: clear, control and retain. The first objective within each of the security districts in the Iraqi capital is to clear out extremist elements neighborhood by neighborhood in an effort to protect the population. And after an area is cleared, we're moving to what we call the control operation. Together with our Iraqi counterparts, we'll maintain a full-time presence on the streets, and we'll do this by building and maintaining joint security stations throughout the city. This effort to re-establish the joint security stations is well under way. The number of stations in each district will be determined by the commanders on the ground who control that area. An area moves into the retain phase when the Iraqi security forces are fully responsible for the day-to-day security mission. At this point, coalition forces begin to move out of the neighborhood and into locations where they can respond to requests for assistance as needed. During these three phrases, efforts will be ongoing to stimulate local economies by creating employment opportunities, initiating reconstruction projects and improving the infrastructure. These efforts will be spear-

---

[5] President George W. Bush, quoted in Kimberly Kagan, "Enforcing the Law: The Baghdad Security Plan Begins," *The Weekly Standard*, February 10–March 5, 2007, p. 2.

headed by neighborhood advisory councils, district advisory councils and the government of Iraq.[6]

By March 2008, implementation of the Baghdad Security Plan had achieved several results that set conditions for the battle in Sadr City. First, al-Qaeda in Iraq had been badly hurt, and its ability to create mass-casualty events significantly reduced. This allowed coalition forces to turn their attention to other destabilizing elements, such as the Sadrist movement. Second, the plan had significantly strengthened the Maliki government's position, enabling it to survive a rupture with the Sadrists. Indeed, Prime Minister al-Maliki was moving to confront the Sadrist militias in Basra, and preparations were well under way by March 2008. Third, coalition forces had largely contained the Jaish al-Mahdi (JAM), the Sadrists' armed militia, to Sadr City, a circumstance that would severely constrain JAM's capabilities in the coming battle.

Moving U.S. troops from their forward operating bases into smaller outposts throughout Baghdad was fundamental to the execution of the Baghdad Security Plan. Key components of the unfolding operations included

- moving U.S. ground forces into Baghdad, where they could directly confront insurgent elements, thereby leading to better local security, cooperation, and human intelligence
- using concrete barriers and checkpoints to
  - limit the ability of insurgents to create mass-casualty events with improvised explosive devices (IEDs), particularly large, vehicle-borne IEDs
  - disrupt the enemy's ability to move freely and resupply its forces
- integrating special operations forces (SOF), conventional forces, and all means of intelligence to locate and kill or capture insurgent leaders
- improving the capability and capacity of Iraqi security forces, including the Iraqi Army and police.[7]

Figure 1 shows the significant reduction in the number of attacks in Baghdad between March 2007 and February 2008.

There was, however, one notable exception to the trend of decreasing levels of violence in Baghdad: Sadr City. The U.S. Army 4th Infantry Division, which was serving as MND-B and commanded by Major General Jeffrey Hammond, had begun to isolate Sadr City to some degree. (See Figure 2 for the dispositions of MND-B's brigade-sized maneuver units.) Within Sadr City's boundaries, however, the militantly anti-American JAM firmly controlled the population. Although SOF and conventional force raids against JAM leadership had resulted in the capture, death, or flight out of Iraq of much of the senior JAM leadership, the raids had also caused significant tension between the Government of Iraq and JAM. Importantly, U.S. activity in Sadr City had largely ceased in October 2007 in the aftermath of an air strike that killed a number of Iraqi civilians. Prime Minister al-Maliki placed Sadr City off limits to U.S. ground operations. JAM's firm control of the population had already severely limited U.S. awareness of what was going on inside Sadr City. After October 2007, U.S. forces were largely blind when it came to the JAM stronghold.

---

[6] Major General Joseph Fil, Jr., quoted in Kagan, "Enforcing the Law," p. 3.

[7] Bill Don Farris II, "Warfighter Observations During the Surge: 2nd Brigade Combat Team, 82nd Airborne Division, 'Task Force Falcon,'" briefing, c. 2008.

Figure 1
Attacks in Baghdad

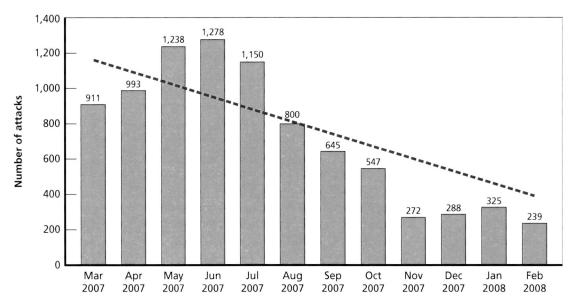

SOURCE: Multi-National Division–Baghdad, "Fort Hood Community Leaders VTC, 25 April 2008," briefing, April 25, 2008.
RAND *OP335-1*

It seems likely that the Maliki government's offensive against militias in Basra, especially JAM, precipitated JAM's own offensive in Baghdad. The Maliki government had been making obvious preparations for the Basra offensive since January 2008, although few U.S. officers seemed either to believe that Prime Minister al-Maliki was serious about the attack or to be aware that it would begin as soon as March 25.

On March 23, 2008, a barrage of rockets fired from Sadr City began hitting targets in Baghdad, including the International Zone (aka the Green Zone), which houses Iraqi government offices and foreign embassies. The March 23 rocket fire appears to have been JAM's initial response to the movement of Iraqi forces toward Basra. Between March 23 and March 25, JAM began to overrun Iraqi checkpoints in and around Sadr City. Other checkpoints were simply occupied by JAM fighters in collusion with their nominal adversaries in the Iraqi police.

The scale of JAM's Sadr City offensive emerged slowly. JAM had fired rockets before. Indeed, it had launched several just a few days earlier, on March 21–22, 2008, according to a company commander in 1st Squadron, 2nd Stryker Cavalry Regiment (1-2 SCR). Taking checkpoints and otherwise intimidating government forces was something JAM forces did more or less continuously. The March offensive's extent became apparent only over several days.

By March 25, however, it had become unmistakably clear that a major battle was now under way. That day, the Government of Iraq launched its offensive in Basra. Al-Sadr therefore publicly ended a self-imposed cease-fire that had been in place since August 2007, and JAM forces throughout Baghdad attacked coalition and government targets with rocket and mortar fire. By the day's end, JAM had overrun about half of the Iraqi security forces checkpoints in and around Sadr City. It also stepped up rocket and mortar attacks against the International Zone. In response, Prime Minister al-Maliki directed coalition forces to stop the rocket attacks and defeat the criminal militias in Sadr City. The Battle of Sadr City was on.

Figure 2
Disposition of MND-B Maneuver Brigades

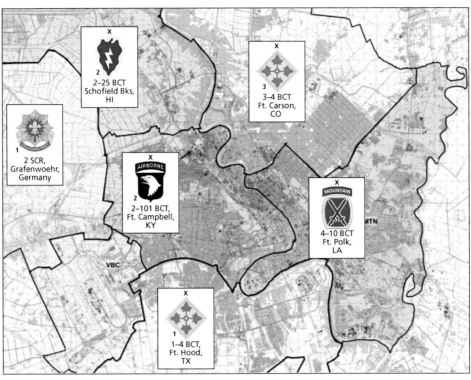

SOURCE: Multi-National Division–Baghdad, "Fort Hood Community Leaders VTC, 25 April 2008."
NOTE: In all, MND-B encompassed more than 31,000 U.S. forces, including six U.S. brigade combat
teams and three additional brigade-sized enabler units. Iraqi forces in Baghdad included three
Iraqi Army divisions (26,000+ forces), two national police divisions (22,000+ forces), the Sons of
Iraq militia (32,000+ forces), and the Iraqi police (20,000+ forces).
RAND *OP335-2*

The Area of Operations

The Battle of Sadr City was centered on the Baghdad district of Thawra, which contains the
neighborhoods of Sadr City, Ishbiliya (which includes the Jamilla Market and is referred to
as such on many U.S. maps), and Habbibiya (also called Thawra on U.S. maps), shown in
Figure 3. The overall Sadr City area spans approximately 35 km², roughly half the size of
Manhattan (which spans 59 km²). At the time of the battle, Sadr City had, by U.S. military
estimates, approximately 2.4 million residents.[8] Figure 3 also shows the location of the International Zone. From the Ishbiliya and Habbibiya neighborhoods below Route Gold (al-Quds
Street), JAM forces were firing 107-mm rockets and mortars into the International Zone. The
Ishbiliya neighborhood also contains the Jamilla Market, Baghdad's largest market east of
the river. Protection money from merchants in this market supplied JAM with much of its

---

[8]   By way of comparison, Manhattan has a population of approximately 1.6 million. The United Nations World Food
Programme (*Comprehensive Food Security and Vulnerability Analysis in Iraq*, Baghdad, 2008, p. 108) estimates Sadr City's
population at that size as well.

Figure 3
The Baghdad International Zone and Sadr City

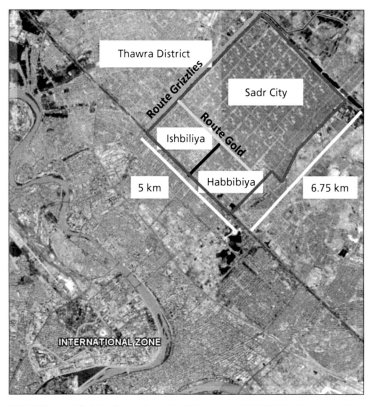

SOURCE: Provided to the authors by C Company, 1-2 SCR (and adapted).
RAND *OP335-3*

resources. Coalition forces also had to combat and contain the Sadrist uprising in the adjacent areas east and north of Sadr City.

Importantly, the International Zone was at the maximum range of the 107-mm rockets and mortars that JAM was firing from its positions below Route Gold. Taking these firing points and pushing JAM above Route Gold would therefore significantly limit JAM's ability to conduct effective indirect-fire attacks against the International Zone.

Mission: Stop the Rockets and Defeat Criminal Militias in Sadr City

As noted earlier, on March 25, Prime Minister al-Maliki directed the Iraqi Army and coalition forces to stop the rocket attacks and defeat the criminal militias in Sadr City. The task fell to Colonel John Hort, commander of the 3rd Brigade Combat Team, 4th Infantry Division (3-4 BCT), within whose area of operations Sadr City fell. Figure 4 shows the overall multinational chain of command in Iraq at the time, including Iraqi security forces units that ultimately became involved in the Battle of Sadr City. Figure 5 depicts the units assigned to 3-4 BCT.

General Hammond focused on going after JAM leaders and on keeping a lid on the rest of Baghdad. Within Sadr City, operations unfolded in four phases as MND-B responded to

Figure 4
The Multinational Chain of Command and Iraqi Security Forces in the 2008 Battle of Sadr City

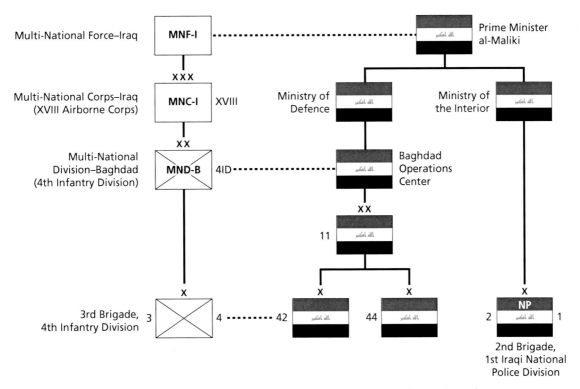

SOURCE: Adapted from 3rd Brigade Combat Team, 4th Infantry Division, "Operation Iraqi Freedom, December 2007–March 2009," briefing, 2009.

RAND OP335-4

Figure 5
3-4 BCT Task Organization as of June 2008

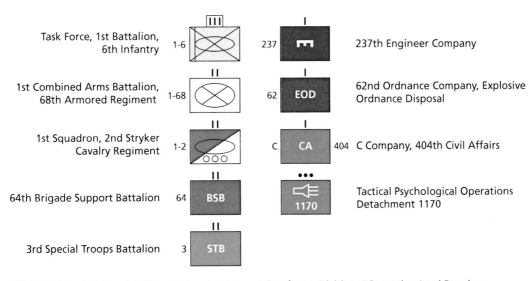

SOURCE: Adapted from 3rd Brigade Combat Team, 4th Infantry Division, "Operation Iraqi Freedom, December 2007–March 2009."

RAND OP335-5

developments. During the first phase, U.S. forces seized control of rocket points of origin south of Route Gold while Iraqi forces attempted to secure the Ishbiliya and Habbibiya neighborhoods. Next, when it became clear that maneuver forces alone could not control JAM's infiltration without a barrier, U.S. forces isolated Ishbiliya and Habbibiya from the rest of Sadr City by building a 12-ft tall wall along Route Gold. JAM more or less exhausted itself contesting the wall's construction. During these first two phases, 3-4 BCT and MND-B employed aerial intelligence, surveillance, and reconnaissance (ISR) and strike assets to neutralize JAM's remaining rocket capability. In the third phase, MND-B exploited the success of its security operations by orchestrating an intensive reconstruction effort. In the final phase, Iraqi security forces, hardened by their earlier fight, occupied the remainder of Sadr City.

The Ground Fight in Sadr City: Heavy Armor Matters

The fight in Sadr City involved two phases: Operation Striker Denial (March 26–April 14) and Operation Gold Wall (April 15–May 15). In the first phase, 1-2 SCR attacked and seized JAM rocket-firing positions in Ishbiliya and Habbibiya while Task Force, 1st Combined Arms Battalion, 68th Armored Regiment (TF 1-68 CAB) quelled the Sadrist uprising in areas west and north of Sadr City proper. Photographs of these operations are presented in Figures 6–8.

When Operation Striker Denial began, U.S. forces immediately encountered JAM forces in prepared positions who were ready and willing to fight. According to U.S. commanders, however, these JAM forces were not able to fight particularly well. Nevertheless, resistance proved tougher than expected. Within a week, the 1-2 SCR lost six of its Stryker vehicles to IEDs and rocket-propelled grenades (RPGs). Colonel Hort decided to reinforce the fight with

Figure 6
1-2 SCR Soldiers and a Stryker Vehicle

SOURCE: Sgt. 1st Class Christina Bhatti, U.S. Army.
RAND OP335-6

Figure 7
Patrolling Sadr City

SOURCE: Public Affairs Office, Multi-National Division–Baghdad, 2008.
RAND *OP335-7*

Figure 8
1-2 SCR Sadr City Patrol

SOURCE: Sgt. 1st Class Christina Bhatti, U.S. Army.
RAND *OP335-8*

heavy armor (M1 Abrams tanks and M2 Bradley fighting vehicles; examples of the former are depicted in Figure 9), and General Hammond surged five additional companies to the 3-4 BCT.

Figure 10 depicts the resulting scheme of maneuver used in Operation Striker Denial, and Figure 11 shows the complex urban environment of Sadr City. Heavy armor proved important in the fight, providing firepower and an ability to withstand hits from IEDs and RPGs. Iraqi security forces joined the fight on April 5 and by April 6 had fought their way to positions near Route Gold. In that fight, conducted more or less independently of U.S. forces, the Iraqi security forces held their positions against incessant JAM attacks. They gained confidence that proved critical in subsequent phases of the battle.

Unfortunately, occupying key terrain below Route Gold did not confer control of those areas to U.S. and Iraqi forces. Unimpeded movement north of Route Gold allowed JAM to assemble and to attack U.S. and Iraqi forces at will. The warren of alleyways and small buildings provided routes for JAM fighters to infiltrate the area below Route Gold. Thus, to hold what they had taken, U.S. and Iraqi forces had to deny JAM its ability to attack at will south of Route Gold. Access to the area below Route Gold was vital to JAM, so it became key terrain for Colonel Hort. Operation Gold Wall, the effort to construct a wall along the length of Route Gold, was intended to deny JAM the ability to operate in Ishbiliya and Habbibiya. This operation is depicted in Figure 12.

In the 30 days of Operation Gold Wall, Colonel Hort's soldiers emplaced some 3,000 12-ft tall, 9-ton T-Wall sections to create a 4.6-km barrier. Figure 13 shows the emplacement of a section of the wall; soldiers, Abrams tanks, and Bradley fighting vehicles protected the effort. JAM fought hard to prevent the establishment of the wall. According to Colonel Hort, the wall, in effect, "became a magnet for every bad guy in Sadr City."[9] As JAM fighters attacked

Figure 9
Abrams Tanks During the Battle of Sadr City

SOURCE: Public Affairs Office, Multi-National Division–Baghdad, 2008.
RAND *OP335-9*

---

[9] "How Technology Won Sadr City Battle: U.S. Military Gives Rare Access to *60 Minutes* in Discussing Aerial Footage and Weaponry," CBSNews.com, October 12, 2008.

Figure 10
Operation Striker Denial Scheme of Maneuver

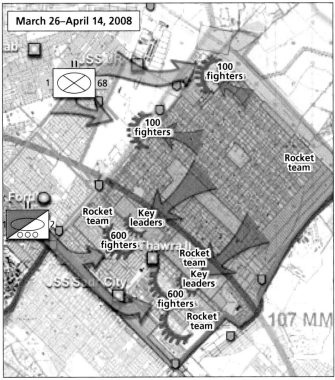

SOURCE: 3rd Brigade Combat Team, 4th Infantry Division, "Operation
Iraqi Freedom, December 2007–March 2009."
NOTE: Orange-shaded areas are suspected or known point-of-origin
sites of rocket launches. JSS UR = Joint Security Station Ur.
RAND OP335-10

to stop completion of the wall, the surrounding area became a killing ground. JAM had few good options. If the wall were completed, it would curtail JAM's access to the population and the market. JAM leaders depended on that access.

Operations Striker Denial and Gold Wall were tough fights, involving three U.S. battalions and Iraqi Security Forces in continuous operations for six weeks.[10] During this period, Abrams tanks and Bradley fighting vehicles were heavily engaged, firing 818 main-gun rounds and 12,091 25-mm rounds against JAM fighters and to detonate IEDs.[11] Additionally, U.S. forces had to constantly adapt to JAM tactics. For example, JAM employed snipers to attempt to knock out the crane that was used to lift the T-Wall sections into place. U.S. forces responded by employing organic U.S. Army and SOF snipers in a countersniper campaign.

As the battle wore on, JAM fighters showed up in ever-decreasing numbers as U.S. and Iraqi forces steadily wore them down. Complementing the conventional fight were efforts by

[10] Task Force, 1st Battalion, 6th Infantry Regiment, joined the fight in Sadr City on May 4 and played a decisive role in combat operations from May 4 to May 15. Its involvement in the battle was critical in relieving some of the pressure on TF 1-68 CAB and 1-2 SCR, and it added heavy armor and partnership capacity to the Iraqi security forces.

[11] 3rd Brigade Combat Team, 4th Infantry Division, "Operation Iraqi Freedom December 2007–March 2009."

Figure 11
A Typical Sadr City Area

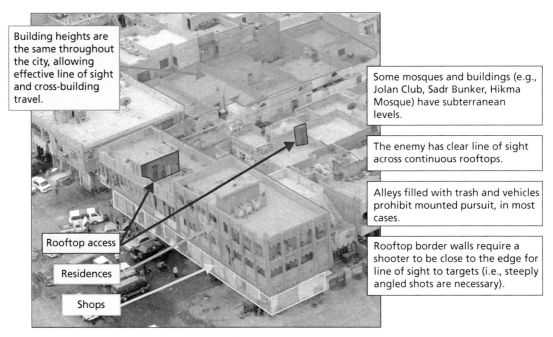

Building heights are the same throughout the city, allowing effective line of sight and cross-building travel.

Some mosques and buildings (e.g., Jolan Club, Sadr Bunker, Hikma Mosque) have subterranean levels.

The enemy has clear line of sight across continuous rooftops.

Alleys filled with trash and vehicles prohibit mounted pursuit, in most cases.

Rooftop border walls require a shooter to be close to the edge for line of sight to targets (i.e., steeply angled shots are necessary).

Rooftop access

Residences

Shops

SOURCE: Provided to the authors by C Company, 1-2 SCR (and adapted).
RAND *OP335-11*

Figure 12
Operation Gold Wall

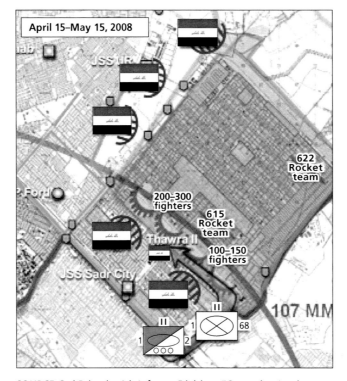

April 15–May 15, 2008

JSS Ur

622 Rocket team

200–300 fighters

615 Rocket team

Thawra II

100–150 fighters

JSS Sadr City

107 MM

SOURCE: 3rd Brigade, 4th Infantry Division, "Operation Iraqi Freedom December 2007–March 2009."
RAND *OP335-12*

**Figure 13
Building the Gold Wall**

SOURCE: Public Affairs Office, Multi-National Division–
Baghdad, 2008.
RAND *OP335-13*

other U.S. government agencies and SOF to hunt and keep the pressure on JAM leaders in Sadr City. Ultimately, six U.S. soldiers died in these operations. JAM lost an estimated 700 fighters, and much of its leadership fled Sadr City for Iran or Syria.[12] On May 11, 2008, al-Sadr asked for another cease-fire.

The Counter-Rocket Fight

As ground maneuver elements fought to isolate Sadr City with the Gold Wall, Colonel Hort and General Hammond were working to stop JAM's indirect-fire attacks on the International Zone. By this point in Operation Iraqi Freedom, Multi-National Corps–Iraq (MNC-I) and MND-B were employing a broad range of U.S. ISR and strike resources in Baghdad. The ISR assets and strike resources deployed in the Battle of Sadr City are depicted in Figure 14, which reproduces a slide briefed by General David H. Petraeus in 2009.

---

[12] For JAM casualties see Paul Webster, "Reconstruction Efforts in Iraq Failing Health," *The Lancet*, Vol. 373, February 21, 2009. According to Webster, municipal officials in Baghdad estimate that the fighting in the Battle of Sadr City killed 925 people and wounded 2,605, an estimate that does not distinguish combatants from noncombatants. Our interviews with U.S. participants in the battle suggest that the number of JAM fighters killed in the battle exceeds 700.

Figure 14
ISR and Strike Assets Employed in the Battle of Sadr City

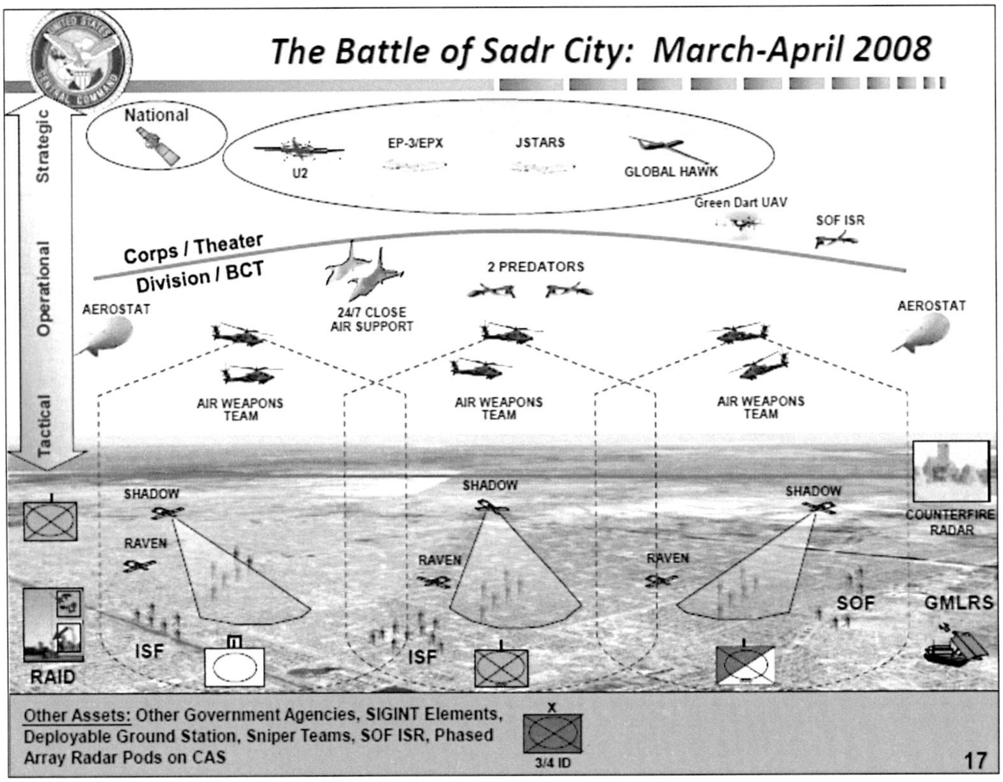

SOURCE: David H. Petraeus, "CENTCOM Update, Center for a New American Security," briefing, 2009.
NOTE: BCT = brigade combat team. CAS = close air support. GMLRS = Guided Multiple Launch Rocket
System. ISF = Iraqi security forces. JSTARS = Joint Surveillance Target Attack Radar System. RAID = Rapid
Aerostat Initial Deployment. SIGINT = signals intelligence. UAV = unmanned aerial vehicle.
RAND OP335-14

Colonel Hort had resources directly allocated to him that were unprecedented for a brigade commander, including two U.S. Air Force MQ-1 Predator unmanned aircraft systems
(UASs) armed with AGM-114 Hellfire missiles (see Figure 15), two U.S. Army RQ-7B Shadow
UASs (see Figure 15), three aerial weapons teams (AWTs) (for a total of six AH-64 Apache
attack helicopters), fixed-wing CAS, and GMLRS—all available 24 hours a day. What was dif-
ferent compared with past practice was the manner in which these resources were employed:
Colonel Hort controlled these assets without having to go through intervening headquarters.
Although most of these systems were used to engage JAM fighters or rockets, on occasion,
large weapons (e.g., 500-lb guided bombs) were used to destroy buildings that were sheltering
snipers. Although there were other fights going on in Iraq and Baghdad, Colonel Hort's fight
in Sadr City was the main effort, and he had priority.

The brigade executed a plan, developed in collaboration with MND-B, in which the BCT
was to focus on JAM fighter and rocket teams while the division continued the attacks on key
leaders—attacks that were of strategic importance to the Government of Iraq, MND-B, and
MNC-I. As was the case in other parts of the battle, the counter-rocket fight was a learning
process.

In his tactical operations center (TOC), Colonel Hort received continuous feeds from
U.S. Air Force Predators (both armed and unarmed) and U.S. Army Shadow UASs. He also

Figure 15
FiMQ-1 Predator and RQ-7B Shadow

SOURCES: U.S. Air Force website (left) and Todd Smith, Deputy Product Manager, Ground Maneuvers Product Office, U.S. Army (right).
RAND *OP335-15*

received information from RAID sensors, counterfire radars, and other ISR assets. His battle staff was able to integrate this information and communicate it to operational units down to the company level via a number of relatively new technologies. For example, they used persistent surveillance and dissemination of systems (PSDS2) to integrate the various sensors. Figure 16 shows an Aerostat, RAID tower, and PSDS2 monitor screens.

Additionally, Colonel Hort was able to communicate in a secure chat room–like environment via secure mIRC and to pass classified information via the SECRET Internet Protocol Router down to the company level.

All of these integrated sensors, communication systems, and strike assets gave 3-4 BCT the ability to find and kill JAM rocket teams and destroy other targets (e.g., mortars). Engagements happened in several ways. First, a radar or other sensor detected a rocket launch. A Shadow UAS was then vectored to the location of the launch and proceeded to follow the target. Finally, a Predator or Apache killed the target. Predators were particularly useful because JAM was expected to have SA-7 man-portable air defense systems and the UASs enabled attacks on JAM without putting Apache crews at risk. Second, skilled intelligence personnel in 3-4 BCT headquarters were tasked with watching the ISR feeds on large screens in the TOC. These individuals were "dedicated scouts" who watched the area under surveillance for enemy activity; when such activity was identified, the process of bringing assets to bear was begun. Before these dedicated scouts were put in place, a "Best Buy" phenomenon was taking place: The activity on the screens was not closely watched by TOC personnel engaged in other activities.[13] Third, ground maneuver forces who detected JAM activity initiated the acquisition and attack processes. What is important is that the brigade commander and his battle staff had these resources pushed down to them—without intervening levels of command and authority—and

---

[13] The Best Buy phenomenon can be experienced by walking through that store's entertainment section on a fall weekend, when many display televisions will be playing football games with the volume muted. Unless one stops and begins to pay attention to a specific display, one will not know who is playing. One must pay attention to a specific screen to see what is happening and to know the score.

Figure 16
Aerostat, RAID Tower, and PSDS2 Monitor Screens

SOURCES: Cpl. Rich Barkemeyer, U.S. Army (top left), U.S. Army (top right),
and Noam Eshel in Defense-Update.com, "Army Deploys 300th RAID Tower,
Supporting Forward Base Protection by Persistent Surveillance and Dissemination
System PSDS2," web page, undated (bottom; used with permission).
RAND OP335-16

could execute mission command. Higher echelons resourced the fight and managed the deeper operations beyond the brigade.

Like the countersniper fight, the counter-rocket fight evolved over time. At first, rocket launch teams were attacked immediately after they had fired. However, the brigade battle staff soon developed "tactical patience" realizing that it was likely hitting only low-level operatives with vehicles and launch rails. Eventually, the staff adopted a best practice of using an ISR platform to "watch the rail" and follow it. When the operatives returned to a supply point or a command location to get additional rockets and instructions, the staff saw the opportunity to strike, hitting not only the operatives but higher elements of the network as well.

Exploitation

MND-B exploited its success in neutralizing JAM with stability operations to secure Ishbiliya and Habbibiya. These efforts were intensified after al-Sadr declared the cease-fire on May 12. Focused reconstruction efforts (see Figure 17) and information operations in those neighbor-

Figure 17
After the Battle, Reconstruction and Cleanup

SOURCE: Public Affairs Office, Multi-National Division–Baghdad, 2008.
RAND *OP335-17*

hoods were intended to influence popular perceptions north of Route Gold as well. Even before fighting subsided completely, U.S. forces resumed applying relentless pressure against JAM's organization. As the reality of JAM's defeat became clearer, the area's inhabitants began providing a flood of reliable intelligence that greatly facilitated this effort.

As the battle subsided, two key realities became apparent to Iraqis living south ("below") the wall along Route Gold. First, Iraqi Army and national police forces were in place and providing security. (Figure 18 depicts Iraqi security forces.) For residents, this harkened back to pre–Operation Iraqi Freedom days: Iraqis were now in charge, and not the coalition forces who would eventually leave Iraq. Second, as security was restored to the area below Route Gold, General Hammond, his subordinate commanders, and the reserve engineer brigade commander working for General Hammond, Brigadier General Jeffrey Talley, began an intense effort to improve conditions below the wall. Much of this was done by enabling Iraqi small businesses, which gave Sadr City's population a stake in the new order. Thus, the population was able to see more permanent progress, and, as conditions improved, the local citizenry became invested in maintaining their security and began providing intelligence to Iraqi and U.S. forces.

When, on May 12, al-Sadr declared a unilateral cease-fire, it is likely that he was simply putting the best face possible on the existing situation. His forces had suffered huge losses, and key leaders had either fled or been killed. The population was growing restive, not only because JAM was perceived as provoking confrontations that resulted in civilian casualties but also because of JAM's depredations. On May 20, unopposed elements of the Iraqi Army's 44th Brigade occupied the remainder of Sadr City.

Figure 18
Iraqi Security Forces

SOURCE: Public Affairs Office, Multi-National Division–Baghdad, 2008.
RAND *OP335-18*

Key Insights from the Fight

The defeat of JAM in Sadr City during the six weeks of high-intensity operations yields several insights that bear highlighting:

- Persistent ISR, technical intelligence, and responsive precision-strike capabilities (afforded by attack helicopters, fixed-wing CAS, UASs, and GMLRS) were fundamental to success and must be integrated. This integration presents significant airspace command and control challenges because multiple aerial platforms and means of direct and indirect fire are being employed in a relatively small area of operations. Nonetheless, these assets are key in showing proportionality and deliberateness, in attacking targets "among the people" with low collateral damage, and in reducing soldier exposure to the risks of urban combat. Finally, relatively large guided bombs (500 lbs or larger) released from fixed-wing aircraft are needed to destroy some categories of urban targets (e.g., multistory buildings).
- Ground maneuver was essential to coalition success in the Battle of Sadr City. It enabled 3-4 BCT to seize control of the fight from JAM. Building the wall along Route Gold was an integral part of ground maneuver. It severely restricted the enemy's ability to employ indirect fire; forced enemy fighters to respond to the increasing isolation that the wall, if finished, would cause; and separated the adversary from the population.
- Heavy forces—i.e., tanks and infantry fighting vehicles—are key elements of maneuver in complex terrain; they are survivable, lethal, and precise.
- Snipers and SOF are important enablers in urban operations and in exploiting intelligence about the location of insurgent leaders.
- The enemy is fleeting, which means that decentralized decisionmaking is required. Units at the brigade level and below must therefore have access to the information and other capabilities required to support the rapid decisions necessary to deal with a highly mobile enemy (which understands its own vulnerabilities) and to enable effective, independent action.
- Capable indigenous security forces are indispensable for securing gains. In the case of Iraqi security forces, it took some time for them to develop competence. Until they did, coalition forces had to both train them and shoulder the bulk of the security challenges.
- A force capable of rapid transitions is important. Soldiers in 3-4 BCT were executing population-centric counterinsurgency (COIN) before the battle of Sadr City. They rapidly transitioned into conducting high-intensity, decentralized, close combat operations and then returned to COIN.

Reimagining Urban Operations as Wide-Area Security Missions

Two general models for dealing with insurgent control of urban areas have become apparent in recent years. The first is the approach taken by the Russian Federation in the Chechen city of Grozny in December 1999–February 2000 and by U.S. forces in the Iraqi city of Fallujah in November 2004. Insurgents in these cities were viewed as cancers that had to be excised. In both of these cases, the cities were essentially besieged and then stormed, a course of action made possible by their geographic isolation. Noncombatants were told to leave before military operations within the cities commenced. Anyone who remained was, in general, viewed as a combatant in what became a block-by-block clearing operation supported by massive amounts of firepower.

Not surprisingly, both cities suffered significant damage. Additionally, casualties among Russian and U.S. forces were high. Although reliable figures are difficult to ascertain, the Russian Federation suffered at least 600 dead (mostly in Grozny, it is assumed) and likely many more wounded in Chechnya between December and early January.[14] In Fallujah, U.S. forces suffered 70 dead and more than 600 wounded.[15] Thus, this model of urban warfare anticipates and accepts extensive collateral damage and relatively high numbers of friendly casualties.

The 2008 Battle of Sadr City offers a second model for wresting control of a city from insurgents: treating an urban area as a wide-area security mission. In Sadr City, unlike in Grozny and Fallujah, telling the civilians to leave what was about to become a high-intensity battlefield simply was not feasible. Sadr City had 2.4 million residents, and there was nowhere for them to go: Sadr City is part of the larger city of Baghdad and, unlike Grozny and Fallujah, is not geographically isolated. These conditions in Sadr City may be representative of the future challenges of urban operations, and they will likely worsen as urban areas around the globe become more densely populated. The objective was not to take and clear Sadr City but to create conditions that would make it both impossible for the insurgents to operate effectively and possible to restore security to the broader population.

Thus, in the Battle of Sadr City, the focus was on enemy fighters and their capabilities. U.S. forces deprived the enemy of the ability to affect events at the operational and strategic levels of war. JAM's control of Sadr City was a perennial problem, but what made its March 2008 offensive problematic was JAM's ability to strike the Green Zone with indirect fires (mainly via rockets). Attacks on the Green Zone threatened to derail the Basra offensive and thereby reveal that the Maliki government was fatally ineffective. However, 3-4 BCT took JAM's offensive capability away by employing determined ground maneuver, which combined infantry and armored vehicles, with support from pervasive ISR and precision-strike capabilities, which were provided by UASs, attack helicopters, artillery, and CAS. Without its indirect-fire capability, JAM could only react locally as coalition forces exploited human and technical intelligence to hunt down its remaining leaders under extremely one-sided conditions.

Finally, Sadr City demonstrates that one of the keys to fighting an urban adversary is to create a situation that will force the enemy to surrender the advantages of the city. This is the art of reimagining urban warfare, and it clearly has doctrinal, organizational, materiel, and training implications for both the U.S. Army and the joint force. In case of the Battle of Sadr City, building the wall along Route Gold threatened to deny JAM access to key terrain and, as Colonel Hort related during an interview with the authors, "agitated the enemy." Quite simply, JAM had to contest the wall or face isolation. In the words of one U.S. officer, the wall was the equivalent of a Roman siege engine about to breach a city's defenses. It created a situation that was intolerable to JAM, and JAM had to come out and fight. In so doing, the enemy attacked U.S. forces that now had the initiative and were in a position of enormous advantage. JAM lost, and the coalition victory in the Battle of Sadr City offers important lessons for the prosecution of future urban operations.

---

[14] Olga Oliker, *Russia's Chechen Wars 1994–2000: Lessons from Urban Combat*, Santa Monica, Calif.: RAND Corporation, MR-1289-A, 2001, pp. 49–50.

[15] Matt M. Matthews, *Operation AL FAJR: A Study in Army and Marine Corps Joint Operations*, Global War on Terrorism Occasional Paper 20, Fort Leavenworth, Kan.: Combat Studies Institute Press, undated, p. 77.

References

3rd Brigade Combat Team, 4th Infantry Division, "Operation Iraqi Freedom, December 2007–March 2009," briefing, 2009.

Cochrane, Marisa, *Special Groups Regenerate*, Washington, D.C.: Institute for the Study of War, 2008.

Cockburn, Patrick, *Moqtada al-Sadr and the Battle for the Future of Iraq*, New York: Scribner, 2008.

Collier, Craig, "Two Cheers for Lethal Operations," *Armed Forces Journal International*, August 2010.

Dawisha, Adeed, "Iraq: A Vote Against Sectarianism," *Journal of Democracy*, Vol. 21, No. 3, July 2010, pp. 26–40.

Defense-Update.com, "Army Deploys 300th RAID Tower, Supporting Forward Base Protection by Persistent Surveillance and Dissemination System PSDS2," web page, undated.

Farris II, Bill Don, "Warfighter Observations During the Surge: 2nd Brigade Combat Team, 82nd Airborne Division, 'Task Force Falcon,'" briefing, c. 2008

"How Technology Won Sadr City Battle: U.S. Military Gives Rare Access to *60 Minutes* in Discussing Aerial Footage and Weaponry," CBSNews.com, October 12, 2008. As of November 1, 2010: http://www.cbsnews.com/stories/2008/10/09/60minutes/main4511800.shtml?tag=contentMain;contentBody

Hughes, Geraint, "The Insurgencies in Iraq, 2003–2009: Origins, Developments and Prospects," *Defence Studies*, Vol. 10, No. 1, May 2010, pp. 152–176.

Kagan, Kimberly, "Enforcing the Law: The Baghdad Security Plan Begins," *The Weekly Standard*, February 10–March 5, 2007.

Matthews, Matt M., *Operation AL FAJR: A Study in Army and Marine Corps Joint Operations*, Global War on Terrorism Occasional Paper 20, Fort Leavenworth, Kan.: Combat Studies Institute Press, undated.

Multi-National Division–Baghdad, "Fort Hood Community Leaders VTC, 25 April 2008," briefing, April 25, 2008.

Oliker, Olga, *Russia's Chechen Wars 1994–2000: Lessons from Urban Combat*, Santa Monica, Calif.: RAND Corporation, MR-1289-A, 2001. As of April 26, 2011: http://www.rand.org/pubs/monograph_reports/MR1289.html

Petraeus, David H., "CENTCOM Update, Center for a New American Security," briefing, 2009.

Stahl, Leslie, "The Battle of Sadr City," *60 Minutes*, October 12, 2008.

United Nations World Food Programme, *Comprehensive Food Security and Vulnerability Analysis in Iraq*, Baghdad, 2008, p. 108.

Webster, Paul, "Reconstruction Efforts in Iraq Failing Health," *The Lancet*, Vol. 373, February 21, 2009.